Charles Rider

Rider's Catskill mountain boarding-house directory and travelers' guide

Charles Rider

Rider's Catskill mountain boarding-house directory and travelers' guide

ISBN/EAN: 9783337208165

Printed in Europe, USA, Canada, Australia, Japan

Cover: Foto ©Andreas Hilbeck / pixelio.de

More available books at **www.hansebooks.com**

RIDER'S

Catskill Mountain

Boarding-House Directory

AND

TRAVELERS' GUIDE.

H. B. HUDLER'S
SUMMER BOARDING-HOUSE.

OPEN JUNE 1st. 1881.

Good boating. bathing and fishing within ¼ mile of house.
FINE WALKS AND DRIVES.

Table well supplied from a large farm attached. Plenty of milk. vegetables. etc. Situated among the highest peaks of the Catskill Mountains: one mile from Mt. Pleasant depot. on Ulster and Delaware Railroad. ¼ mile from Post-office.

NO MOSQUITOES! NO MALARIA!

For terms etc., apply to

H. B. Hudler,
The Corner, Ulster Co., N. Y.

RIDER'S

Catskill Mountain

BOARDING-HOUSE DIRECTORY

AND

TRAVELERS' GUIDE.

PART FIRST:

BOARDING-HOUSE DIRECTORY.

PART SECOND:

TRAVELERS' GUIDE.

Charles H. Rider,

AUTHOR AND PUBLISHER,

BUSHNELLSVILLE, GREENE CO., N. Y.

—1881—

CAUTION.

EDITED AND PUBLISHED

BY

Charles H. Rider,

BUSHNELLSVILLE, GREENE COUNTY, NEW YORK.

1881.

INTRODUCTION.

THE CATSKILL MOUNTAINS for years have been visited by those seeking rest and enjoyment from the busy cares of city life, and have found the mountain air so bracing and healthful, and the location so enjoyable in every way, as to far exceed the Sea-shore resorts.

The thousands who annually visit the Catskills, accord in pronouncing these mountain resorts as the "Switzerland of America."

It is my object to give a full list of all Boarding Houses and Hotels, on and among the Catskills, so as to aid the visitor in selecting from its complete list, the desired place of resort.

The Guide apartment will be found full of instructive tables. The distances given are compiled from the latest official sources, and actual measurements by the Author.

This Book will be issued yearly, and revised and corrected when necessary. Is not intended as an advertising cajole, nor a novel story-book of the Catskills, of things read of and never seen, but, a standard Directory and Guide, for travelers and others.

> Those golden hills, the mountain's brace
> E'er since the Devonian age,
> And now the traveler seeks his rest
> Beneath the golden stage.
>
> C. H. R.

ERRATA.

ADDITIONS AND CORRECTIONS.

BOARDING-HOUSE DIRECTORY.

EXPLANATIONS TO DIRECTORY.

Directory is arranged as follows: 1st. Name of individual or firm. 2d. Post office address. 3rd. The number of persons each individual or firm can accommodate in A. D. 1881.

☞ When writing parties named, please mention seeing the address in RIDER'S DIRECTORY.

Name and Post-office address.	Can accommodate.
Anderson, Chas., Catskill, Greene Co., N. Y.	—
Badeau, James H., Catskill, Greene Co., N. Y.	—
Bailey, O. T., Jewett Heights, Greene Co., N. Y.	30
Bassett, C. L., South Cairo, Greene Co., N. Y.	14
Beckwith, Z., Cairo, Greene Co., N. Y.	40
Behm, P. L., Catskill, Greene Co., N. Y.	—
Bennett, J. N., South Durham, Greene Co., N. Y.	10
Bergner, John, Catskill, Greene Co., N. Y.	—
Bloodgood, Mrs. M., Union Society, Greene Co., N. Y.	30
Boice, J. N., Shokan, Ulster Co., N. Y.	15
Boice, N., Shokan, Ulster Co., N. Y.	10

Name and Post-office address.	Can accommodate.
Burget, Jacob, Catskill, Greene Co., N. Y.	—
Burgher, J. M., West Shokan, Ulster Co., N. Y.	20
Calkins, M. B., East Durham, Greene Co., N. Y.	20
Cherritree, John H., Oak Hill, Greene Co., N. Y.	10
Cole, Harmon, South Cairo, Greene Co., N. Y.	—
Dean, J. P., Cairo, Greene Co., N. Y.	—
Dederick, Chas., Kiskatom, Greene Co., N. Y.	20
Dederick, Geo., Cairo, Greene Co., N. Y.	—
Dederick, Hez., Palenville, Greene Co., N. Y.	—
Dodge, R., Freehold, Greene Co., N. Y.	20
Dunham, Lewis P., Spruceton, Greene Co., N. Y.	25
Eckler, Wm., East Durham, Greene Co., N. Y.	25
Feeney, Daniel, Gayhead, Greene Co., N. Y.	30
French, W. O., East Durham, Greene Co., N. Y.	15
Fullegar, Robert N., Leeds, Greene Co., N. Y.	—
Garrison, Charles, Bushnellsville, Greene Co., N. Y.	30
Gay, P. C., Catskill, Greene Co., N. Y.	—
Goetchins, P. M., Catskill, Greene Co., N. Y.	150
Goodwin, John, Palenville, Greene Co., N. Y.	—
Hack, L., Catskill, Greene Co., N. Y.	—
Hallenbeck, P. W., Tannersville, Greene Co., N. Y.	75
Hawver, H., Palenville, Greene Co., N. Y.	40
Hawver, P., Palenville, Greene Co., N. Y.	40
Hedges, Geo., East Durham, Greene Co., N. Y.	—

Name and Post-office address.	Can accommodate.
Hine, Selden H., Cairo, Greene Co., N. Y	35
Holbert, F. J., Cat-kill, Greene Co., N. Y	35
Hoos, H. V., Freehold, Greene Co., N. Y	—
Hotel, Burger's, Palenville, Greene Co , N. Y	35
Houghtaling, J. S., Prattsville, Greene Co., N. Y	40
House, Summit, Pine Hill, Ulster Co., N. Y	500
Jennings, D. W., Cairo, Greene Co., N. Y	40
Jennings, E. T., Freehold, Greene Co., N. Y	—
Jennings, James, East Durham, Greene Co., N. Y	20
Johnson, Mrs., Acra, Greene Co., N. Y	15
Jones, Andrew P., Cairo, Greene Co., N. Y	20
Lawrence, R. M., Kiskatom, Greene Co., N. Y	25
Lennon, W. N., Cairo, Greene Co., N. Y	—
Locke, F., Cairo, Greene Co., N. Y	15
McCabe, H. J., Greenville, Greene Co., N. Y	20
McGiffert, John, Leeds, Greene Co., N. Y	—
McGiffert, Joseph, Leeds, Greene Co., N. Y	30
McGiffert, Robert, Leeds, Greene Co., N. Y	—
Mead, W. D., Leeds, Greene Co., N. Y	—
Milner, Mrs., Acra, Greene Co., N. Y	15
Olney, Geo. R., Catskill, Greene Co., N. Y	20
Overbaugh, Jas. P., Catskill, Greene Co., N. Y	30
Peckham & Rapelyea, Prattsville, Greene Co., N. Y	50
Person, H. A., Catskill, Greene Co., N. Y	100

Name and Post-office address.	Can accommodate.
Plush, Philip, Catskill, Greene Co., N. Y	60
Potter, W. J., Acra, Greene Co., N. Y	15
Redcliffe, East Durham, Greene Co., N. Y	100
Roraback, J. H., Lexington, Greene Co., N. Y	25
Salisbury, James, Catskill, Greene Co., N. Y	30
Sax, Frederick, Kiskatom, Greene Co., N. Y	35
Schutt, J. L., Catskill, Greene Co., N. Y	150
Signer, I. T., Kiskatom, Greene Co., N. Y	35
Simpkins, S. L., Leeds, Greene Co., N. Y	12
Soper, John, Windham, Greene Co., N. Y	30
Spoor, Mrs. A. A., Freehold, Greene Co., N. Y	20
Smith, E. P., Freehold, Greene Co., N. Y	15
Stoddard, J. H., Cairo, Greene Co., N. Y	25
Stryker, M. A., Prattsville, Greene Co., N. Y	50
Summit House, Pine Hill, Ulster Co., N. Y	500
Teale, Theodore C., Palenville, Greene Co., N. Y	100
Travis, James H., Gayhead, Greene Co., N. Y	12
Van Loan, Van Ness, Catskill, Greene Co., N. Y	12
Van Valkenburg, A., Windham, Greene Co., N. Y	12
Vincent, Mrs. L. E., Freehold, Greene Co., N. Y	25
Waldron, John, East Durham, Greene Co., N. Y	30
White, Wm., East Durham, Greene Co., N. Y	30
Winans, Seymour, Kiskatom, Greene Co, N. Y	20
Wright, Alphas, Cairo, Greene Co, N. Y	35

TYPOGRAPHICAL ERRORS.

On page 33, 1st line, 2d word—Azoic; it should of said Eozoic.

On page 31, 17th line, 10th word—nature; it should of said water.

CONTENTS.

Catskill Mountain

BOARDING-HOUSE DIRECTORY.

~~~~

EXPLANATIONS TO DIRECTORY.

Directory is arranged as follows: 1st. Name of individual
or firm. 2d. Post office address. 3rd. The number of persons each individual or firm can accommodate in A. D. 1881.
☞ When writing parties named please mention seeing the
address in RIDER'S DIRECTORY.

Name and Post-office address.	Can ac-commodate.
Ackerly House, Margaretville, Delaware Co., N. Y.	100
Ackerly, Wm., Arkville, Delaware Co., N. Y.	10
Adams, Daniel J., Brodhead, Ulster Co., N. Y.	25
Allaben, O. M., Margaretville, Delaware Co., N. Y.	40
Allen, Sherman, Olive, Ulster Co., N. Y.	10
Alton, Wm., Griflin's Corners, Delaware Co., N. Y.	10
Andrus, D. D., Roxbury, Delaware Co. N. Y.	15
Atwater, Mrs. E., Hunter, Greene Co., N. Y.	10
Austin, Geo., Kiskatom, Greene Co., N. Y.	25

Name and Post-office address.	Can accommodate.
Baker, J., Olive, Ulster Co., N. Y.	15
Baldwin, A, G., Gilboa, Schoharie Co., N. Y.	12
Banker, T C, Griffin's Corners, Delaware Co., N. Y.	25
Barber, F. A, Lanesville, Greene Co., N. Y.	25
Barritt, Thos , Griffin's Corners, Delaware Co., N. Y.	25
Bartlett, A. F., Stamford, Delaware Co., N. Y.	60
Beach, Chas. A , Catskill, Greene Co , N. Y.	400
Beach, F., Hunter, Greene Co., N. Y.	12
Bear, Chas , Catskill, Greene Co., N. Y.	25
Becker, W H., Gilboa, Schoharie Co., N. Y.	15
Beekman, James, Woodstock, Ulster Co , N. Y.	15
Benham, C. K., Prattsville, Greene Co., N. Y.	12
Beets, Mrs. H. P., Gilboa, Schoharie Co., N. Y.	6
Bechler, Jacob, Griffin's Corners, Delaware Co., N. Y.	30
Berryam, Jas. H., Brodhead, Ulster Co., N. Y.	10
Berry, Ira, Lake Hill, Ulster Co., N. Y.	4
Biddell, H. E., Hunter, Greene Co., N. Y.	15
Bishop, Moses, Brown's Station, Ulster Co., N. Y.	15
Blish, J. M., Griffin's Corners Delaware Co., N. Y.	20
Blodget, C. C., Pine Hill, Ulster Co., N. Y.	30
Bloom, David, Catskill, Greene Co., N. Y.	50
Bloom, Isaac S., Brodhead, Ulster Co., N. Y.	25
Boice, Wm. V. N., Boiceville, Ulster Co., N. Y.	6
Boughton, Avery, Halcott, Greene Co., N. Y.	15

13

Name and Post-office address.	Can accommodate.
Bouton, G. M., Roxbury, Delaware Co., N. Y.	20
Brewster, H. D., South Gilboa, Schoharie Co., N. Y.	10
Brockway, E. G., Stamford, Delaware Co., N. Y.	20
Brodhead, C. Case, Brodhead, Ulster Co., N. Y.	20
Brodhead, J. L., Brodhead, Ulster Co., N. Y.	12
Brodhead, Stephen H., Brodhead, Ulster Co., N. Y.	20
Britt, Peter, Kiskatom, Greene Co., N. Y.	30
Britt, Sen., Wm., Kiskatom Greene Co., N. Y.	10
Brothers', Walter, Cario, Greene Co., N. Y.	50
Brower, Geo., Olive, Ulster Co., N. Y.	12
Brown, Albert, Brown's Station, Ulster Co., N. Y.	20
Brown, Mrs. J., Tannersville, Greene Co., N. Y.	50
Brown, Nicholas, Shandaken, Ulster Co., N. Y.	25
Brownell, R. S., Stamford, Delaware Co., N. Y.	12
Bryant, E., Lumberville, Delaware Co., N. Y.	40
Buckingham, Mrs. C., Gilboa, Schoharie Co., N. Y.	10
Burger, Peter, Palenville, Greene Co., N. Y.	50
Bush, H. C., Olive, Ulster Co., N. Y.	6
Campbell, Geo., Tannersville, Greene Co., N. Y.	25
Castel, A. A., West Hurley, Ulster Co., N. Y.	4
Chamberlain, S. C., Lexington, Greene Co., N. Y.	36
Chase, Geo. H., Jewett, Greene Co., N. Y.	20
Chichester, John, South Gilboa, Schoharie Co., N. Y.	10
Churchill, A. L., Stamford, Delaware Co., N. Y.	25

Name and Post-office address.	Can ac-commodate.
Churchill, S. E., Stamford, Delaware Co., N. Y.	40
Clark, J. R., Stamford, Delaware Co., N. Y.	15
Coe, O. R., Windham, Greene Co., N. Y.	40
Cole, Geo., Pine Hill, Ulster Co., N. Y.	—
Cole, S., Arkville, Delaware Co., N. Y.	30
Connelly, Amos, Phœnicia, Ulster Co., N. Y.	18
Connelly, Abram, Phœnicia, Ulster Co., N. Y.	10
Conrow, Robert, South Gilboa, Schoharie Co., N. Y.	30
Conrow, Stephen, South Gilboa, Schoharie Co., N. Y.	10
Cooper, William, Bearsville, Ulster Co., N. Y.	15
Cornell, Grant &., Catskill, Greene Co., N. Y.	300
Cornish, B. F., Pine Hill, Ulster Co., N. Y.	8
Crispell, N. B., West Shokan, Ulster Co., N. Y.	10
Crosby, O. B., Lanesville, Greene Co., N. Y.	16
Davis, Charles H., Olive, Ulster Co., N. Y.	6
Davis, David F., West Shokan, Ulster Co., N. Y.	10
Davis, Dewitt C., Shokan, Ulster Co., N. Y.	10
Davis, Geo., Roxbury, Delaware Co., N. Y.	5
Davis, H. W., Boiceville, Ulster Co., N. Y.	20
Davis, J., Olive, Ulster Co., N. Y.	15
Davis, N. K., Olive, Ulster Co., N. Y.	12
Davis, O., Shokan, Ulster Co., N. Y.	20
Davis, Oliver, Brodhead, Ulster Co., N. Y.	10
Decker, L., Prattsville, Greene, Co. N. Y.	20

Name and Post-office address.	Can ac-commodate.
Dedrick, Egbert, Brown's Station, Ulster Co., N. Y	20
Desilva, W. J., Lumberville, Delaware Co., N. Y	20
Devasego House, Prattsville, Greene Co., N. Y	50
Deyoe, A., Lexington, Greene Co., N. Y	20
Deyoe, R. C., Lexington, Greene Co., N. Y	30
Deyoe Bros., Westkill, Greene Co., N. Y	75
Dickson, M., Brushland, Delaware Co., N. Y	8
Dickson, W. H., Lumberville, Delaware Co., N. Y	10
Douglass, Mrs. R. M., Lexington, Greene Co., N. Y	60
Douglass, Wm. A., Hunter, Greene Co., N. Y	15
Dubois, C., Palenville, Greene Co., N. Y	80
Dubois, John, Shokan, Ulster Co., N. Y	20
Dudley, John M., Roxbury, Delaware Co., N. Y	15
Dunnigan, Francis, Shokan, Ulster Co., N. Y	15
Dutcher, Byron, Big Indian, Ulster Co., N. Y	10
Eckert, James M., Shokan, Ulster Co., N. Y	10
Eckert, Talmadge, West Shokan, Ulster Co., N. Y	10
Eckert, Thompson, West Shokan, Ulster Co., N. Y	10
Eckler, H. S., Catskill, Greene Co., N. Y	50
Eggleston, G. N., Tannersville, Greene Co., N. Y	40
Eighmey, Daniel S., Lake Hill, Ulster Co., N. Y	4
Elmendorf, A. F., Olive, Ulster Co., N. Y	15
Elmendorf, Albert, Olive, Ulster Co., N. Y	20
Elmendorf, Alexander, Woodstock, Ulster Co., N. Y	15

Name and Post-office address.	Can accommodate.
Elmendorf. D. E., Olive, Ulster Co., N. Y	10
Elmendorf, Mrs. F., Olive, Ulster Co., N. Y	10
Elmendorf, Wm., Olive, Ulster Co., N. Y	10
Elvyn, Peter B., Woodstock, Ulster Co., N. Y	10
Enderlin, C. J., Roxbury, Delaware Co., N. Y	12
Ennis, Geo., Shandaken, Ulster Co., N. Y	30
Ennist, J., Shokan, Ulster Co. N. Y	15
Everett. B., Olive, Ulster Co., N. Y	15
Ferguson. D. W., Prattsville, Greene Co., N. Y	15
Fisk. Mrs. E., Griffin's Corners, Delaware Co., N. Y	10
Floyd, Mrs. Chas., Pine Hill, Ulster Co., N. Y	60
Foote, W. S., Hobert, Delaware Co., N. Y	10
Ford, Chas. L., Tannersville, Greene Co., N. Y	60
Ford, Dr. S. L., Westkill, Greene Co., N. Y	30
France, Willis, Pine Hill, Ulster Co., N. Y	15
Frazer, C. O., South Gilboa, Schoharie, Co., N. Y	10
Frisbee, W. M., South Gilboa, Schoharie Co., N. Y	10
Gaylord. John B., Stamford, Delaware Co., N. Y	12
Glennon, Owen, Palenville, Greene Co., N. Y	75
Goodnough, Lyman, Stamford, Delaware Co., N. Y	4
Goodrich, Mrs., Hunter, Greene Co., N. Y	16
Goodwin, C. L., Palenville, Greene Co., N. Y	25
Goodwin, Edwin E., Palenville, Greene Co., N. Y	25
Grant, D. B., Hobert, Delaware Co., N. Y	15

Name and Post-office address.	Can accommodate.
Grant, W. B., Hobert, Delaware Co., N. Y	6
Green, Wm. F., Hunter, Greene Co., N. Y	10
Griffin, B., Hobert, Delaware Co., N. Y	15
Griffin, D. C., West Hurley, Ulster Co., N. Y	18
Griffin, D. W., Griffin's Corners, Delaware Co., N. Y	20
Griffin, H. A., Gilboa Schoharie Co., N. Y	12
Griffin, John B., Stamford, Delaware Co., N. Y	12
Griffin, Mrs. C. J., Big Indian, Ulster Co., N. Y	4
Griffeth, Henry, Shandaken, Ulster Co., N. Y	15
Guigou, Augustus, Pine Hill, Ulster Co., N. Y	200
Hagadorn, Addison, Gilboa, Schoharie Co., N. Y	15
Hagadorn, Frank, Gilboa, Schoharie Co., N. Y	30
Haines, Aaron, Tannersville, Greene Co., N. Y	25
Haines, Abram, Tannersville, Greene Co., N. Y	15
Haines, Charles, Tannersville, Greene Co., N. Y	100
Haines, C. W., Catskill, Greene Co., N. Y	80
Haines, George, Palenville, Greene Co., N. Y	18
Haines, J. E., Tannersville, Greene Co., N. Y	30
Haines, Jesse, Tannersville, Greene Co., N. Y	15
Haines, Jermiah, Tannersville, Greene Co., N. Y	10
Haines, John J., Tannersville, Greene Co., N. Y	20
Haines, Miles, Tannersville, Greene Co., N. Y	50
Haines, Uriah, Tannersville, Greene Co., N. Y	26
Hamilton, J., Stamford, Delaware Co., N. Y	20

Name and Post-office address.	Can accommodate.
Hamilton, O. J., Shandaken, Ulster Co., N. Y	10
Hamma, R., Roxbury, Delaware Co., N. Y	15
Hardenburgh, M. J., West Hurley, Ulster Co., N. Y	25
Hasbrouck, B. E., Lake Hill, Ulster Co., N. Y	16
Hasbrouck, J. L., Pine Hill, Ulster Co., N. Y	25
Hatfield, Mrs., Griffin's Corners, Delaware Co., N. Y	65
Hazard, J. M., Gilboa, Schoharie, Co., N. Y	10
Hemsley, Mrs. Alex., Tannersville, Greene Co., N. Y	50
Hewitt, Arnold, Griffin's Corners, Delaware Co., N. Y	8
Hicks, C. L., Roxbury, Delaware Co., N. Y	25
Hill, Jr., Thomas, Shandaken, Ulster Co., N. Y	25
Hinman, Mrs. A. E., Palenville, Greene Co., N. Y	25
Hitt, R. E., Union Grove, Delaware Co., N. Y	20
Hogaboom, H., Lexington, Greene Co., N. Y	15
Hollister, Lewis, Olive, Ulster Co., N. Y	12
Hoofman, Benjiman, Woodstock, Ulster Co., N. Y	15
Hoofman, P. F., Arkville, Delaware Co., N. Y	10
Hotel, Devoe Bros., Westkill, Greene Co., N. Y	75
Hotel, Geo. Cole, Pine Hill, Ulster Co., N. Y	—
Hotel, Gunn's, Catskill, Greene Co., N. Y	75
Hotel, Overlook, Woodstock, Ulster Co., N. Y	200
Hotel, Prospect Park, Catskill, Greene Co., N. Y	400
House, Ackerly, Margaretville, Delaware Co., N. Y	100
House, Breeze Lawn, Hunter, Greene Co., N. Y	100

Name and Post-office address.	Can accommodate.
House, Catskill mountain, Catskill, Greene Co., N. Y.	400
House, Clinton, Tannersville, Greene Co., N. Y.	150
House, Cockburn, Long Year, Ulster Co., N. Y.	75
House, Delaware, Stamford, Delaware Co., N. Y.	20
House, Devasego, Prattsville, Greene Co., N. Y.	50
House, Grand View, Cario, Greene Co., N. Y.	50
House, Grand View, Lake Hill, Ulster Co., N. Y.	30
House, Grant, Catskill, Greene Co., N. Y.	300
House, Guigou, Pine Hill, Ulster Co., N. Y.	200
House, Hunter, Hunter, Greene Co., N. Y.	75
House, Irving, Catskill, Greene Co., N. Y.	100
House, Laurel, Catskill, Greene Co., N. Y.	125
House, Mansion, Rondout, Ulster Co., N. Y.	50
House, Margaretville, Margaretville, Delaware Co., N. Y.	25
House, Moresville, Moresville, Delaware Co., N. Y.	25
House, Overlook, Woodstock, Ulster Co., N. Y.	200
House, River Side, Margaretville, Delaware Co., N. Y.	40
House, Shady Lawn, Westkill, Greene Co., N. Y.	45
House, Shandaken, Shandaken, Ulster Co., N. Y.	50
House, Tremper, Phœnicia, Ulster Co., N. Y.	275
Hommell, P. M., Davenport, Delaware Co., N. Y.	10
Hommell, Peter, Bushnellsville, Greene Co., N. Y.	8
Houtaling, J. S., Prattsville, Greene Co., N. Y.	60
Howland, A., Boiceville, Ulster Co., N. Y.	8

Name and Post-office address.	Can accommodate.
Hubbard, D. H., Westkill, Greene Co., N. Y	25
Hubbell, P. F., Roxbury, Delaware Co., N. Y	25
Hudler, H. B., The Corner, Ulster Co., N. Y	30
Hughes, Ira J., Andes, Delaware Co., N. Y	20
Hull, Dr. A. C., Olive, Ulster Co., N. Y	15
Hull, John, Boiceville, Ulster Co., N. Y	15
Hull, Mrs. D., Margaretville, Delaware Co., N. Y	15
Hunt, Hiram P., Delhi, Delaware Co., N. Y	6
Hyzer, Ira W., Andes, Delaware Co., N. Y	10
Ingols, Frederick, Tannersville, Greene Co., N. Y	25
Ives, S. P., Margaretville, Delaware Co., N. Y	20
Jackson, Mrs. Thomas, Catskill, Greene Co., N. Y	20
Johnson, Abram, Griffin's Corners, Delaware Co., N. Y	15
Johnson, F., Phœnicia, Ulster Co., N. Y	10
Jones, Geo. H., Griffin's Corners Delaware Co., N. Y	24
Judson, Jr., J., Prattsville, Greene Co., N. Y	40
Kelly, H. B., Arkville, Delaware Co., N. Y	80
Kendall, Sarah E., Stamford, Delaware Co., N. Y	18
Kipp, I. Lexington, Greene Co., N. Y	30
Krom, Jacob, Shokan, Ulster Co., N. Y	16
Krom, Nelson, West Shokan, Ulster Co., N. Y	25
Lake, A. & V. D., The Corner, Ulster Co., N. Y	35
Lake, C. H., Tannersville, Greene Co., N. Y	30
Lament, F. B., Shandaken, Ulster Co., N. Y	60

Name and Post-office address.	Can ac- commodate.
Lament, J., Lexington, Greene Co., N. Y	11
Lament, T. S., Pine Hill, Ulster Co., N. Y	20
Lamoreau, A., East Windham, Greene Co., N. Y	40
Lamson, C. M., The Corner, Ulster Co., N. Y	40
Lamson, Mrs. S., The Corner, Ulster Co., N. Y	40
Lane, Albert, Lake Hill, Ulster Co., N. Y	12
Lane, Edward, Phœnicia, Ulster Co., N. Y	25
Lasher, David, Pine Hill, Ulster Co., N. Y	25
Lasher, M. A., Arkville, Delaware Co., N. Y	40
Lasher, Philip, Pine Hill, Ulster Co., N. Y	12
Lasher, Philip H., Brown's Station, Ulster Co., N. Y	50
Law, J. A., Meridith, Delaware Co., N. Y	15
Lawler, John, Shandaken, Ulster Co., N. Y	30
Lawrence, S., Kiskatom, Greene Co., N. Y	25
Laymon, Edgar, Tannersville, Greene Co., N. Y	20
Laymon, H. A., Tannersville, Greene Co., N. Y	40
Lee, Wallace, Olive, Ulster Co., N. Y	15
Lemmon, D. T., Palenville, Greene Co., N. Y	25
Leonard, D. C., Prattsville, Greene Co., N. Y	20
Leonard, Mrs. G. H., Stamford, Delaware Co., N. Y	8
Lindsley, Lewis, Hunter, Greene Co., N. Y	25
Locke, Hugh, Olive, Ulster Co., N. Y	8
Lockwood, Jacob S., Brown's Station, Ulster Co., N. Y	20
Lockwood, J. S., Brodhead, Ulster Co., N. Y	12

Name and Post-office address.	Can ac-commodate.
Lockwood, S. C., Fergusonville, Delaware Co., N. Y.	10
Longyear, A., Woodstock, Ulster Co., N. Y.	10
Longyear, I. W., Arkville, Delaware Co., N. Y.	30
Loomis, A. P., Hunter, Greene Co., N. Y.	8
Lutz, A., Prattsville, Greene Co., N. Y.	10
Maben, Wm., Lexington, Greene Co., N. Y.	20
Manison, M. C., Bearsville, Ulster Co., N. Y.	16
Markle, Andrew, Olive, Ulster Co., N. Y.	10
Markle, Mrs. C., Olive, Ulster Co., N. Y.	5
Markle, S., Shokan, Ulster Co., N. Y.	6
Marrison, Alex., Griffin's Corners, Delaware Co., N. Y.	12
Marsh, M. G., Prattsville, Greene Co., N. Y.	20
Martin, H. A., Lexington, Greene Co., N. Y.	70
Martin, S., Lexington, Greene Co., N. Y.	20
Mathews, E. R., West Shokan, Ulster Co., N. Y.	10
Maybe, Egbert, Big Indian, Ulster Co., N. Y.	12
Mayham, B. S., South Gilboa, Schoharie Co., N. Y.	12
Mayham, C. H., South Gilboa, Schoharie Co., N. Y.	10
Mayham, L. D., South Gilboa, Schoharie Co., N. Y.	10
Maylan, Geo., Olive, Ulster Co., N. Y.	15
Maynard, A. A., Stamford, Delaware Co., N. Y.	8
Maynard, J. W., Stamford, Delaware Co., N. Y.	25
McMurray, Mrs. J., Margaretville, Delaware Co., N. Y.	20
McMurray, John, Delhi, Delaware Co., N. Y.	10

Name and Post-office address.	Can accommodate.
Mc Kee, J. H., Stamford, Delaware Co., N. Y	14
Mc Killip, J. P., Halcottville, Delaware Co., N. Y	10
Meade, Geo., Woodstock, Ulster Co., N. Y	40
Meagher, M. A., Arkville, Delaware Co., N. Y	10
Merritt, Chas. D., Cario, Greene Co., N. Y	50
Meyer, D. H., Prattsville, Greene Co., N. Y	20
Miiler, John, Bearsville, Ulster Co., N. Y	20
Miller, Mrs. J. S., Bearsville, Ulster Co., N. Y	10
Misner, Thomas, Pine Hill, Ulster Co., N. Y	10
Montgomery. T. E., Woodstock, Ulster Co., N. Y	8
Moore, Geo. B., Stamford, Delaware Co., N. Y	12
More, L. P., South Gilboa, Schoharie Co., N. Y	10
More, O. P., Roxbury, Delaware Co., N. Y	20
More, W. P., Moresville, Delaware Co., N. Y	8
Mosher, S. A., Lake Hill, Ulster Co., N. Y	30
Mott, Geo. C., Acra, Greene Co., N. Y	50
Mower, L. W., Leeds, Greene Co., N. Y	30
Munger, Sherman, Windham, Greene Co., N. Y	75
Mulford, S. S., Tannersville, Greene Co., N. Y	150
Mulnix, A. R., Big Indian, Ulster Co., N. Y	15
Newton, W. C., Phœnicia, Ulster Co., N. Y	15
Newcombe, C. R., Prattsville, Greene Co., N. Y	40
O'Conor, Francis, Clarks Factory, Delaware Co., N. Y	8
O'Hara, B., Lexington, Greene Co., N. Y	225

Name and Post-office address.	Can accommodate.
O'Hara, John, Tannersville, Greene Co., N. Y.	25
O'Neil, Thomas, Phœnicia, Ulster Co., N. Y.	65
Osterhoudt, Henry, Palenville, GreeneCo., N. Y.	25
Osterhoudt, Mrs. M., Lumberville, Delaware Co., N. Y.	40
Ostrander, C., Shandaken, Ulster Co., N. Y.	40
Peck, A. E., Downsville, Delaware Co., N. Y.	6
Peck, Philo, Palenville, Greene Co., N. Y.	100
Peck, Philo P., Palenville, Greene Co., N. Y.	20
Pettit, Mrs. Rachel, Lexington, Greene Co., N. Y.	10
Phillips, E., Olive, Ulster Co., N. Y.	8
Phillips, David, Lake Hill, Ulster Co., N. Y.	5
Phillips, I. D., Phœnicia, Ulster Co., N. Y.	15
Plattner C. H. Q., Prattsville, Greene Co., N. Y.	20
Plue, Z., Lake Hill, Ulster Co., N. Y.	15
Pond, Emmons, Jewitt Hights, Greene Co., N. Y.	50
Powell, John, Roxbury, Delaware Co., N. Y.	8
Powell, W. D., Roxbury, Delaware Co., N. Y.	25
Preston, D. W., Phœnicia, Ulster Co., N. Y.	15
Quick, Abram, Lake Hill, Ulster Co., N. Y.	12
Quick, Lewis, Hunter, Greene Co., N. Y.	10
Randall, S. S., The Corner, Ulster Co., N. Y.	8
Randall, T., The Corner, Ulster Co., N. Y.	2
Rappleyea, Peckham &, Prattsville, Greene Co., N. Y.	75
Reade, George, Tannersville, Greene Co., N. Y.	30

Name and Post-office address.	Can accommodate.
Reader, Paul, Prattsville, Greene Co., N. Y.	125
Reilly, L., Jefferson, Schoharie, Co., N. Y.	10
Reynolds, Dr. James, Hobert, Delaware Co., N. Y.	16
Richmyer, H., Gilboa, Schoharie Co., N. Y.	15
Richmyer, J. H., Gilboa, Schoharie Co., N. Y.	8
Rider, John, Tannersville, Greene Co., N. Y.	30
Riley, Chris., Westkill, Greene Co., N. Y.	40
Risley, A. N., Woodstock, Ulster Co., N. Y.	15
Robinson, A. S., Prattsville, Greene Co., N. Y.	15
Robinson, G. F., Roxbury, Delaware Co., N. Y.	8
Roe, Hiram, Tannersville, Greene Co., N. Y.	25
Roggen, Aaron, Tannersville, Greene Co., N. Y.	150
Roney, Miss N. A., Roxbury, Delaware Co., N. Y.	6
Rowe, Geo. E., West Hurley, Ulster Co., N. Y.	4
Rowland, I. N., Roxbury, Delaware Co., N. Y.	15
Rudolph, W., Prattsville, Greene Co., N. Y.	15
Rulifson, F. G., Stamford, Delaware Co., N. Y.	12
Rusk, James & Son, Hunter, Greene Co., N. Y.	65
Rusk, Wm. G., Hunter Greene Co., N. Y.	65
Russell, Thos. B., Brushland, Delaware Co., N. Y.	4
Sanford, Mrs. E. J., Margaretville, Delaware Co., N. Y.	30
Sax, Geo., Prattsville, Greene Co., N. Y.	40
Saxe, Frederick, Catskill, Greene Co., N. Y.	35
Schumacher, W. H., The Corner, Ulster Co., N. Y.	50

Name and Post-office address.	Can accommodate.
Scott, S. F., Margaretville, Delaware Co., N. Y.	50
Scribner, P. H., Palenville, Greene Co., N. Y.	100
Scribner, Nelson, Tannersville, Greene Co., N. Y.	25
Scutt, L. J., Tannersville, Greene Co., N. Y.	100
Sellick, Solomon, Gilboa, Schoharie Co., N. Y.	10
Shaffer, W. B., Shavertown, Delaware Co., N. Y.	30
Shaw, Daniel W., Delhi, Delaware Co., N. Y.	12
Shaw, Herbert, Brodhead, Ulster Co., N. Y.	4
Sheldon, E. C., Davenport, Delaware Co., N. Y.	15
Sherman, M. E., East Windham, Greene Co., N. Y.	30
Short, Charles, Lake Hill, Ulster Co., N. Y.	16
Short, David P., Brown's Station, Ulster Co., N. Y.	25
Shutts, L., Roxbury, Delaware Co., N. Y.	10
Simmons, A., Olive, Ulster Co., N. Y.	15
Simpson, Geo., Stamford, Delaware Co., N. Y.	20
Simpson J., Phœnicia, Ulster Co., N. Y.	20
Sliter, G. R., Halcottville, Delaware, Co., N. Y.	10
Smith, Chârles, Pine Hill, Ulster Co., N. Y.	10
Smith, John, Lexington, Greene Co., N. Y.	20
Smith, J. S., Big Indian, Ulster Co., N. Y.	15
Smith, Mrs. Jane, Olive, Ulster Co., N. Y.	6
Smith, Mrs. Thos., Pine Hill, Ulster Co., N. Y.	8
Smith, R. S., Roxbury, Delaware Co., N. Y.	10
Smith, T. S., Roxbury, Delaware Co., N. Y.	15

Name and Post-office address.	Can accommodate.
Snyder, Edgar, Woodstock, Ulster Co., N. Y	8
Snyder, O., Woodstock, Ulster Co., N. Y	1
Soule, S. D., Shandaken, Ulster Co., N. Y	10
Southard, Smith, Gilboa, Schoharie, Co., N. Y	12
Sowles, E. A., South Gilboa, Schoharie Co., N. Y	15
Spencer, Peter V., Palenville, Greene Co., N. Y	10
Spencer, M. D., Gilboa, Schoharie Co., N. Y	10
Spencer, M. F., Stamford, Delaware Co., N. Y	4
Staples, E. D., Lake Hill, Ulster Co., N. Y	12
Stephens, Geo. A., Hobart, Delaware Co., N. Y	15
Stevens, Mrs. E., South Gilboa, Schoharie Co., N. Y	10
Stevenson, E. H., Andes, Delaware Co., N. Y	10
Stoutenberg, Mrs. Jennie, Olive, Ulster Co., N. Y	10
St. John, Mrs. A. G., Downsville, Delaware Co., N. Y	6
Stratton, Addison, Brown's-Station, Ulster Co., N. Y	20
Stryker, M. H., Prattsville, Greene Co., N. Y	70
Thompson, J. S., Lexington, Greene Co., N. Y	30
Thompson, Sylvester, Woodstock, Ulster Co., N. Y	15
Thrope, G. M., Windham, Greene Co., N. Y	15
Todd, D. & O., Turnwood, Ulster Co., N. Y	16
Van, Alex., Griffin's Corners, Delaware Co., N. Y	12
Van De Bogert, H. P., Lake Hill, Ulster Co., N. Y	12
VanGaasbeck, Mrs. M., Olive, Ulster Co., N. Y	6
VanHovenberg, Cyrus, Olive, Ulster Co., N. Y	10

Name and Post-office address.	Can accommodate.
Van Loan, W. T., Hunter, Greene Co., N. Y.	100
Van Pelt, M. C., Hunter, Greene Co., N. Y.	100
VanValkenbergh, Alex., Halcott, Greene Co., N. Y.	15
VanValkenbergh, A. T., Spruceton, Greene Co., N. Y.	25
VanValkenbergh, W., Spruceton, Greene Co., N. Y.	20
Vermilyea, O., Griffin's Corners, Delaware Co., N. Y.	30
Warne, Fred, Stamford, Delaware Co., N. Y.	8
Washburn, J. H., Andes, Delaware Co., N. Y.	10
Waters, J. G., Lake Hill, Ulster Co., N. Y.	15
Webster, J. B., Cario, Greene Co., N. Y.	30
Weidner, C. H., West Shokan, Ulster Co., N. Y.	25
White, T. E., Downsville, Delaware Co., N. Y.	10
Whitcomb, Horace, Lexington, Greene Co., N. Y.	30
Whitney, Giles, Shandaken, Ulster, Co., N. Y.	35
Whitney, Jacob, Shandaken, Ulster Co., N. Y.	25
Whittaker, L., Hunter, Greene Co., N. Y.	12
Wilhmot, Mrs. J., Lake Hill, Ulster Co., N. Y.	12
Winans, H. W., Shokan, Ulster Co., N. Y.	10
Winchell, Hiram J., Brown's Station, Ulster Co., N. Y.	25
Winchell, Isaac, Olive, Ulster Co., N. Y.	10
Winchelsea, The, Palenville, Greene Co., N. Y.	40
Windrum, John, Shokan, Ulster Co., N. Y.	16
Winne, C. C., West Shokan, Ulster Co., N. Y.	30
Winne, D., The Corner, Ulster Co., N. Y.	60

Name and Post-office address.	Can ac-commodate.
Winne, Mrs. C. M., West Shokan, Ulster Co., N. Y	15
Winter, D. T., Pine Hill, Ulster Co., N. Y	20
Wolven, P. A., Boiceville, Ulster Co., N. Y	15

☞ For additions and corrections see Errata, following the Introduction.

GEOLOGICAL ESSAY
— ON THE —
Cobble-Stones of the Catskills.

. ———

How came they in their present condition?—What is their
history?—Can we learn anything by studying
their geological formation?

———

BY W. H. DYMOND.

———

We stumble over them, we kick them out from under
our thoughtless feet and call them bad names, and we who
have been reared among the Catskills even begrudge the
mauger ground they occupy. The above questions involve
more real knowledge than the writers brain contains.

So wonderful is the history, and so sublime is the study of
the little insignificant looking cobble-stone that the most
towering genius of the nineteenth century can not even
write the title page of its contents. The questions not only
involves the physical condition of the stone, but by fair rea-
soning it carries us back to a time when it formed a part of

the great underlying rock of the globe. If we could know the true chemical analyses of its constituent parts, it would carry us away back into illimitable space beyond the *Nebula* birth of our noble planet when its particles were floating as atoms through universal space.

The cobble-stone was once a part of the solid rock which composes the geological formation of the Devonian group of the Catskills; and is composed of sand, grit, and silicon combined with oxygen, which are the principle ingredients of all rocks except the limestone. It was during the Devonian period that the contraction of the earths crust caused the upheaval of our grand old Catskills, and the various geological formations were broken up. The dips, contortions, and falling of older rocks over younger formations, delineate the certainty of general confusion.

The mountains rose, upborne by the force of interior heat sending millions of tons of fragments into the valleys below; these being exposed for hundreds of thousands of centuries to the action of water have worn to cobbles, pebbles and sand, giving us our rock soil thickly interspersed with cobble-stones.

We should not be much surprised when we are told that geological investigation teaches that the entire crust of the earth has been deposited as sediment at the bottom of the ocean, at one time covering the whole face of the globe: and the more we become acquainted with its crust, the more apparent it is that fire and water have been the two great agents of creation.

The astronomer may gaze upon the rolling worlds around him, and view with awe and delight the midnight vault over his head and contemplate the majesty of the universe; while the geologist takes up the cobble-stone which is trampled under foot, and presents it to us as a chapter in the *Great Volume of Nature* which we may read with satisfaction and profit, the inspiration of which has never been disputed.

All other books are held under the scrutiny of challenge

and have been tampered with more or less by deceitful human hands. By reading the volume of nature we may safely discover how our noble planet came into its present condition. The cobble-stone, the pebble, and each grain of sand, speaks to us in indisputable language the inspiration of the Hand which wrote it.

From the cobble-stone we learn that water has been an active agent in bringing it to its present rounded form. It was once a part of a solid rock which has been broken off and rolled over and over in the water till it acquired its present shape. I see in the cobble-stone several pebbles of various colors; some of them belong to the fire made rocks of the granitic period, others to the metamorphic formation. This proves beyond a doubt that in the immensely distant past the whole earth was in an intensely heated condition, in fact, a molten mass; and rocks of immense thickness from time to time cooled the fiery contents long before nature existed on its surface. No other theory can possibly account for the dreadful physical condition of the horid *Mauvais T. rres*; or "Bad Lands" of the North-west, without coming to the natural conclusion that the earth was originally a fiery mass, and that its interior at present is one vast ocean of fire.

This hypothesis teaches us how naturally our earth came into its present condition, and gives us reason for a thousand facts that came under our observation, otherwise dark and mysterious. As far as geological investigation has gone, there has been found about sixty-three natural eliments dispersed through nature, and of these the earth is composed.

It is said that one-half of the earths crust is composed of oxygen and invisible gas. This doubtless is the moving cause of attraction, and attraction beyond a doubt is the cause of the spheroidical figure of our earth, and this great principle of attraction which is stamped on all the matter of the universe, doubtless is the cause whereby all bodies by a circular fortuitous concourse of atoms continually attract each other, under the influence of attraction all bodies and parts tend naturally to their center. The cobble-stone has more in it than I have already hinted.

Let us examine it more closely!

What are those singular marks and impressions eradiating from its surface? It is a fossil, and what are fossils? We answer, animals or vegetables buried in the earth by natural causes, and preserved; as stony indications of their existence are found in the rocks. They may be animals almost unchanged, or bones, or impressions of forms in the rocks produced by the infiltrating of silica through the interstices, thus reducing to solid stone whatever comes in contact with the petrifying waters common to those ages when fire and water were contesting each others rights to rule absalutely.

Fossils are more than I have already hinted, they are letters in which the worlds history is written; and without their assistance we should not have known the past history of our planet, a matter of the greatest importance.

Certain forms of life lived at certain times, and their remains became buried in the sediment deposited during those times. About twenty thousand fossils have already been found in all of the stratified rocks above the metamorphic. Fossils are of the greatest importance, for with their assistance we are able to deside the comparitive ages of rocks, take away these and we should have to group our way through darkness which oracle nor science could penetrate.

The cobble-stone is not a mere isolated letter, but it is a whole chapter in the great volume of nature: in it are the tissues of the fraimwork of the globe, in it are the first germ of creation.

Let us examine it again, it contains the form of the first born of our earth, it gives us a history of the induction of that wonderful and misterious phenomena called life. It is not an animal or a vegetable, it occupies an intermedial point between the three kingdoms, mineral, animal and vegetable, its radiating arms reach away down the stream of time to the Azoic Age or Dawn of life, beyond that all is fire and chaotic confusion. The impressions we see in the cobble-stone is the Rock Writing Protozoan of the Devonian rocks of the Catskills; it was an animal common to that age, and was hastening on to assimulate into the naked reed-like trees of the Carboniferous period. In the coal measures we do see the impress of an animal, but we see the vegetable it foreshadowed.

But where and when did life begin?

It did not begin on the mountain, for the earths crust was to thin to bear the weight of mountains. It did not begin on the land, for that was one vast wilderness of heated rock and life was as impossible on its surface as in a fiery furnace.

What is that curious looking thing we see away down at the bottom of the Laurentian ocean struggling in the hot mud? It is the *Radiata* or "*Plant Animal*," and it runs so low into the mineral kingdom that it is difficult to tell where the one begins or the other leaves off. This was the first an lowest form of life, and was a distant prophecy of the countless millions that should join in the march of life's grand procession up the evolving scale.

Following that misterious thing called life, along the march of ages, we not only discover the scale of evolution, but the wonderful adaptation of each stage of existence to answer the end of creation.

It was during the Devonian Age, when the Catskill moun-tains rose above the dark waters of the universal ocean.

The cobble-stones which are so profusely scattered over the land in the vicinity of the Catskills, are as records of the six independant forms of life as they appeared during the Devonian Age.

> Count the millions of years that passed,
>   Before these mountains rose,
> And then, turn to the present day,
>   The tourist's, grand and sweet repose.

RIDER'S
CATSKILL MOUNTAIN
BOARDING-HOUSE DIRECTORY

AND

Travelers' Guide;

The ONLY BOOK on the CATSKILLS that gives a
COMPLETE LIST of HOTELS and BOARDING-HOUSES
and the number of persons each house can accommodate.

GIVING, ALSO,

Car, Steam-Boat and **Carriage** *ROUTES*, and *RATES* of
FARE FROM NEW YORK CITY
—TO THE—

Catskill Mountains.

This book contains numerous tables giving the distances
from New York City to all points of the Catskill Mountains.

Tables giving the distances from **four of the highest
mountains** of the Catskills, to all their circumambient peaks.

The four tables are so arranged as to enable any stranger
of the mountains, to locate and define the numerous mountains and peaks as seen from the four "Kings" of this
"Switzerland of America."

New and various essays, descriptive notes, and other val-
uable information will also appear in future editions.

PUBLISHED YEARLY, PRICE, 25 CENTS.

Advertisements inserted at low rates. Any additional information given free by addressing the Author.

Charles H. Rider,
BUSHNELLSVILLE, GREENE CO., N. Y.

TRAVELERS' GUIDE,

—WITH—

DISTANCE TABLES

—AND—

Car, Steam-Boat and Carriage Routes and Rates of Fare

—FROM—

New York City

—TO ALL POINTS OF THE—

CATSKILL MOUNTAINS.

—ALSO—

Tables giving the distances from the SLIDE, HUNTER. EAGLE and BLACK DOME MOUNTAINS, (Four of the highest mountains of all the Catskills) to all their circumambient mountains and peaks in the Catskills.

☞ The four tables of the mountains are so arranged as to enable a stranger to locate and define the numerous mountains and peaks as seen from the *four* named towering "Kings of the Catskills," either of which are over 4,000 feet above tide water.

TABLE OF ALTITUDES OF THE CATSKILLS.

Time Tables of the Various Routes. Telegraph Rates.
etc., etc.

———

—1881—

PREFACE.

The Catskill Mountains for years have been an enticing Summer resort. The city people, whose health have been much impaired by the close confinement and busy cares of city life: come here to seek rest, improve health, and enjoy themselves: and it is yet to be reported of any one coming to the mountains under those expectations and returning home disappointed or dissatisfied.

It is my object, after having spent twenty-four years among the pleasant valleys, towering hills and lofty mountains of the Catskills, to explain as briefly and correctly as possible, the various routes, distances, Car, Steam-boat, Carriage and Telegraph Rates to all points of the Catskill Mountains. The numerous Descriptive Notes, Essays, Tables etc., found in this apartment, is hoped, by the Author, to aid the tourists in their travels to the "everlasting towers" of the Catskills. Having gained access to the peaks of the highest mountains, (many of which are unknown to the thousands who annually visit the Catskills, and return home thinking they have seen "all")—and using the highest trees thereon for an observatory—I saw the beautiful valleys, deep gorges, lofty hills and towering mountains on all sides, the view extending over an area of over 1,200 square miles, or the entire group of the Catskills. The views thus noted, I shall endeavor to describe in this apartment "new" mountains, many of which are of great interest, surpassing many of those that have become famous.

Ever willing to wield my pen in explanation of the never ending grandeur of these "everlasting hills." I send forth to the people this small pamphlet as a correct guide to all points of the Catskill Mountains—my native home.

C. H. R.

DISTANCES
From NEW YORK CITY to SUMMER RESORTS
IN THE NORTH-EAST PART OF THE

CATSKILLS

Via CATSKILL LANDING, CATSKILL, NEW YORK.

☞ Ticket to Catskill *via* New York Central and Hudson River Railroad, at Grand Central Depot; or Steamer "City of Catskill" or "Escort," at Pier 34, foot of Harrison Street; or Albany Day Boats, at Vestry Street Pier, New York.

NAME OF P. O.	MILES FROM N. Y.	NAME OF P. O.	MILES FROM N. Y.
Acra	122	Haines's Falls	123
Ashland	139	Hunter	129
Athens	114	Leeds	113
Cairo	119	Lexington	134
Catskill	109	Oak Hill	131
Cooksburgh	132	Palenville	119
Conesville	140	Potter's Hollow	135
Durham	131	Prattsville	145
East Durham	124	Red Falls	142
East Windham	128	South Cairo	117
Forge	119	South Durham	125
Freehold	124	Tannersville	125
Gilboa	150	Union Society	132
Grand View Mt. House	118	Windham	136

CHARLES GARRISON, Bushnellsville, Greene Co., N. Y.

PLEASANT HOME.

Situated 2¾ miles from Shandaken *depot*, on the banks of one of the finest Trout Streams in the Catskills. Only two miles to the celebrated DEEP HOLLOW NOTCH, Eagle and Balsam Mountains. A short distance from Post-office—four mails daily. Terms reasonable. Address as above.

FARE

From NEW YORK CITY to SUMMER RESORTS

IN THE NORTH-EAST PART OF THE

CATSKILLS

Via CATSKILL LANDING, CATSKILL, NEW YORK.

☞ Take Steamer "City of Catskill" or "Escort," at Pier 34, Foot of Harrison St., N. Y., at 6 o'clock P. M., Daily (Sundays excepted.)

☞ The RATES given below are for THROUGH TICKETS ONLY.

NAME OF P. O.	FARE FROM N. Y.
Acra................$2.00	*Haines's Falls........$2.00
Ashland.............2.50	Hunter................2.00
Athens..............1.25	Leeds.................1.25
Cairo...............1.75	Lexington.............2.00
Catskill............1.00	Oak Hill..............2.00
Cooksburgh..........2.00	Palenville............2.00
Conesville..........3.00	Potter's Hollow.......2.25
Durham..............2.00	Prattsville...........2.50
East Durham.........2.00	Red Falls.............2.50
East Windham........2.50	South Cairo..........1.75
Forge...............1.75	South Durham..........2.00
Freehold............2.00	Tannersville..........2.50
Gilboa..............3.00	Union Society.........2.50
*Grand View Mt. House..2.00	Windham...............2.50

☞ To ascertain Car Rates, add $1.73 to above rates, and purchase tickets via N. Y. C. & H. R. R. R., at Grand Central Depot, New York. R. R. Tickets to Catskill only.

*Not a Post-office. Through Tickets to Catskill only.

THE CATSKILLS.

BY HARRY HOWE.

"Touched by a light that hath no name,
The gold-fringed mountains rise;
And through the glowing morning clouds,
The rore mist, lifts and flies."

WE feel safe in claiming the Catskill Mountains as one of
the greatest attractions in America, and deserves all the
praises bestowed upon them. Summed up in the briefest
way possible, the picturesque scenery of the Catskills have
a world-wide reputation, and are unexcelled by any place
on this globe, either in healthfulness of climate or beauty of
location.

The tools used in finishing this portion of the Empire
State, left the face of the country in a rough condition.
Such "plowing without much harrowing" there must have
been to turn up such ridges like these mountains! Among
the furrows we find rugged gorges, hugh rocks, beautiful
water-falls, wandering streams, peaceful lakes, delicate
ferns, mosses and flowers, immense trees, and wonderful
prospects that can never be forgotten.

However great their anticipations may be, few visitors are
ever disappointed in these mountains; thousands of tourists
annually come here to pass the heated term, and always go
away satisfied.

Scattered promiscuously among the Catskills are a large
number of well-known and well-patronized resorts, capable
of accommodating from 25 to 500 guests each comfortably.
There houses are pleasantly situated, and most of them command excellent views of the mountains and valleys. The
rooms are spacious and airy, and the proprietors have a
wide fame for the abundance and excellence of their tables,
the prompt and courteous attention to guests, and the care

(Continued on page 42.)

GLEN HALL

☞ For a description of this pleasantly situated SUMMER RESORT see next page.

GLEN HALL,

PINE HILL, ULSTER COUNTY, N. Y.

The Most Attractive Locality in the

Catskill Mountains.

(1.660 FEET ABOVE TIDE-WATER.)

Directly on the Ulster and Delaware Railroad; ½ mile from
Pine Hill station and Telegraph office—four mails daily—
and yet in the midst of the most attractive mountain scenery
in the State. Objects of interest are reached in every direc-
tion, over pleasant Mountain and Valley Roads.

The brooks are filled with Trout, and the woods with game.
The locality invites equally the Sportsman, the Pleasure
Seeker, and the Invalid.

GLEN HALL has unusually large and well ventilated rooms,
extensive verandas, surrounded by pleasant grounds, and is
in every way calculated to afford an agreeable *Summer Home*.

NO MOSQUITOES! NO MALARIA!!

Accommodations Superior.   TERMS:—$8. to $10. per week.

Reduction to Children and Nurses.

Address

Mrs. Chas. Floyd,

PINE HILL, ULSTER COUNTY, N. Y.

ROUTE:—Take Steamer Cornell or Baldwin, from Pier
34 N. R., foot of Harrison Street, N. Y., at 4 P. M., to Rondout; or Albany Day Boats, from Vestry Street Pier; or N.
Y. C. & H. R. R. R., leaving Grand Central depot at 11.03
A. M., to Rhinebeck, thence by ferry to Rondout, connecting
with Ulster and Delaware Railroad Express trains, arriving
at Pine Hill 10.15 A. M., and 4.58 P. M.

taken to satisfy those that partake of their hospitality. The prices for board vary from $1.00 to $3.50 per day; $6.00 to $20.00 per week; Reductions are made for long term guests, and children and servants. The season begins about June 1st, and closes in October. A few houses accommodate guests the year round.

Knowing tourists invariably assert that there are no resorts so romantic, so bracing, so enjoyable in nearly every way, as are these mountain resorts, with their facilities for hunting, fishing and bathing, and their cool healthful atmosphere.

SPRUCETON.

THE location of Spruceton hamlet command fine views of the Westkill valley and its surrounding mountains. The hamlet took its name from the large amount of Spruce timber that has from time to time been taken from the mountains in that vicinity. Spruceton is but three miles from Westkill village, Church and Telegraph office. Ten miles from Shandaken depot, on Ulster and Delaware Railroad.

The route to the depot is very romantic, unsurpassed by any route in this part of the Catskills.

Brookside Cottage,

SPRUCETON, GREENE CO., N. Y.

This COTTAGE is 2,000 feet above tide-water, and is situated on the banks of the Westkill Creek. Good Trout fishing and hunting. Pleasant walks and drives.

TELEGRAPH AND POST-OFFICE NEAR.

TERMS: - - - $6. @ $8. per week.

Address, **A. T. VAN,** as above

MILES FROM NEW YORK

TO THE FOLLOWING

SUMMER RESORTS AMONG THE CATSKILLS.

☞ See next page for a description of **ROUTES, RATES** of **FARE, &c.**

NAME OF P. O.		MILES FROM N. Y.	
Arkville	136	Olive	101
Bearsville	107	Phœnicia	115
Big Indian	124	Pine Hill	127
Bushnellsville	124	Prattsville	158
Clovesville	134	Red Falls	165
Griffin's Corners	133	Rondout	88
Halcottville	141	Roxbury	148
Hunter	129	Sampsonville	112
Hurley	96	Shandaken	121
Jewett Centre	135	Shokan	105
Jewett Heights	137	Spruceton	131
Kingston	90	Tannersville	133
Lake Hill	118	The Corner	113
Lanesville	120	West Hurley	97
Lexington	132	Westkill	128
Long Year	112	West Shokan	107
Margaretville	137	Woodland	120
Moresville	154	Woodstock	104

TELEGRAPH RATES.

The cost of sending a message from any part of the Catskill mountains to New York city, is, 25 cents for the first 10 words, and two cents for each additional word, except Lexington, Westkill and Shandaken Company's line, the charges on this line are 40 cents for the first 10 words, and three cents for each additional word.

RATES OF FARE FROM NEW YORK,

VIA STEAMERS "CORNELL" AND "BALDWIN,"
from Pier 34, foot of Harrison Street, N. Y.,

TO THE FOLLOWING

SUMMER RESORTS AMONG THE CATSKILLS.

☞ Purchase *THROUGH TICKETS.*

Andes	$3.25	Lexington	$2.50
Arkville	2 44	Mount Pleasant	1.72
Big Indian	2.08	Olive Branch	1.36
Bloomville	3.50	Phœnicia	1.81
Boiceville	1.63	Pine Hill	2.20
Brodhead's Bridge	1.54	Rondout	1.00
Brown's Station	1.45	Roxbury	2.77
Delhi	3.25	Shandaken	1.99
Fox Hollow	1.96	Shokan	1.54
Gilboa	3.25	South Gilboa	3.13
Grand Gorge	2.95	Stamford	3.22
Griffin's Corners	2.32	Summit	2.26
Halcottville	2.59	West Hurley	1.31
Hunter	2.50	Westkill	2.40

☞ To ascertain Car Rates, add 88 cents to above rates, and purchase tickets via New York Central and Hudson River Railroad, at Grand Central Depot, New York;* or Erie and Wallkill Valley Railroad, from Jersey City, N. J.‡

☞ Through tickets by either route.

---

*Stop at Rhinebeck, take ferry to Rondout, thence by Ulster and Delaware Railroad.

‡Change cars at Rondout.

DISTANCE TABLE.

SLIDE MOUNTAIN

—TO ALL ITS CIRCUMAMBIENT—

CATSKILL PEAKS.

EXPLANATIONS.

Arc 1st. South to West.   Arc 2d. North to West.   Arc 3rd. North to East.   Arc 4th. South to East.

ARC 1st.

DEGREES.		MILES.
0.	Mt. Peakamoose	3¾

ARC 2d.

2.	Bloomburg Mountain	27
8.	Eagle Mountain	15
10.	Irish Mountain	30
11.	Bald Mountain	33
12.	Summit Hill	14
13.	Mt. Utsyanthia	36
14.	Summit Depot	14
28.	Balsam Mountain	11
36.	Pakataghkan Mountain	18
57.	Big Indian Mountain	7½

ARC 3rd.

0.	Round Top	26
1.	Panther Mountain	6¼
3.	Pine Mountain	31

DEGREES.		MILES.
4.	Vly Mountain	20
9.	Mt. Royal	30
10.	Balsam High Peak	14
10.	Vinegar Hill	21
12.	Mt. Sherrill	12
13.	Huntersfield Mountain	32
15.	Lost Mountain	32
17.	Ashland Pinnacle	32
20.	Tower Mountain	24
22.	North Dome	12
22.	Mt. Richmond	33
25.	Richtmyer Peak	33
27.	Mount Pisgah	34
30.	Mount Hayden	33
34.	Ginseng Mountain	32
36.	Mount Zoar	32
42.	Windham High Peak	37
43.	Colonel's Chair	20
45.	Thomas Cole	28
46.	Black Dome	29
50.	Hunter Mountain	19
50.	Parker Mountain	24
52.	Black Head	30
57.	Plateau Mountain	29
58.	Cario Round Top	33
61.	North Mountain	28
62.	Round Top	24
64.	High Peak	25
67.	Sugar Loaf	19
69.	Mount Tremper	9
70.	Twin Mountain	20
73.	Indian Head	21
82.	Overlook Mountain	21

ARC 4th.

34. Hanover Mountain............................4¾
39. High Point................................4½
65. Mt. Cornell,...............................2¼
65. Blackberry Point...........................6
66. *Kingston City*............................26
82. Cross Mountain.............................5
85. Wittenberg Mountain,.......................2¾

HENRY GRIFFETH, Shandaken, Ulster County, N. Y.

In the very midst of the Catskills. Thirty-three miles from Rondout, on Ulster and Delaware Railroad. House pleasantly located, ½ mile from depot. Grounds extend to Esopus Creek and are well shaded. Fine mountain scenery; pure mountain air; pleasant walks and drives. Rooms large, airy and pleasant. Plenty of eggs, milk and poultry. *Accommodations good in all respects. Terms reasonable.*

No chills and fever! NO MOSQUITOES! NO MALARIA!! - - - - Address as above.

SIMPSON HOUSE.
Is well located. Drainage good.

ABOUT TEN MINUTES WALK FROM PHŒNICIA STATION, on Ulster and Delaware Railroad.

TERMS REASONABLE.

For further information apply to

James A. Simpson,
Phœnicia, Ulster County, N. Y.

DISTANCE TABLE.

HUNTER MOUNTAIN
—TO ALL ITS CIRCUMAMBIENT—
CATSKILL PEAKS.

EXPLANATIONS.

Arc 1st, South to West. Arc 2d, North to West. Arc 3rd, North to East. Arc 4th, South to East.

ARC 1st.

DEGREES.		MILES
7.	Mt. Tobias	10
16.	High Point	21
29.	Mt. Tremper	10
30.	Mt. Pleasant	13
35.	Hanover Mountain	20
40.	Wittenberg Mountain	18
40.	Mt. Cornell	20
40.	Mt. Peakamoose	23
50.	Slide Mountain	19
62.	Mt. Sheridan	9
62.	Panther Mountain	15
80.	Balsam Mountain	19
85.	North Dome	9
86.	Mt. Sherril	11

ARC 2d.

7.	Mt. Richmond	17
10.	Colonel's Chair	2

DEGREES.		MILES
15.	Ashland Pinnacle	18
18.	Lost Mountain	19
21.	Huntersfield Mountain	20
29.	Tower Mountain	12
29.	Mt. Royal	21
35.	Pine Mountain	22
43.	Mt. Utsyanthia	31
44.	Bald Mountain	27
45.	Irish Mountain	25
47.	Round Top	19
47.	Bloomberg Mountain	20
58.	Vly Mountain	14
78.	Eagle Mountain	12
80.	Balsam High Peak	9
88.	Summit Hill	17
88.	Pakataghkan Mountain	24

A R C 3rd.

0.	Richmyer Peak	17
7.	Mt. Pisgah	16
9.	Mt. Hayden	15
15.	Ginseng Mountain	14
20.	Mount Zoar	13
30.	Windham High Peak	12
40.	Thomas Cole	9
40.	Acra Point	12
43.	Parker Mountain	5
43.	Black Dome	9
57.	Black Head	9
70.	Cario Round Top	14
81.	North Mountain	9

A R C 4th.

37.	Overlook Mountain	11

DEGREES.	MILES
46. Sugar Loaf	5
65. Plateau Mountain	3
81. High Peak	8
82. Round Top	7
83. South Mountain	9

DISTANCE TABLE.

EAGLE MOUNTAIN

—TO ALL ITS CIRCUMAMBIENT—

CATSKILL PEAKS.

EXPLANATIONS.

Arc 1st, South to West.   Arc 2d, North to West.   Arc 3rd, North to East.   Arc 4th, South to East.

ARC 1st.

Degrees.	Miles.
28. Big Indian Mountain	11
40. Balsam Mountain	7
60. Summit Hill	4
84. Pakataghkan Mountain	10

ARC 2d.

0. Bloomberg Mountain	12
12. Irish Mountain	16
17. Bald Mountain	18
20. Mt. Utsyanthia	22

A R C 3rd.

DEGREES.	MILES
5. Round Top	11
20. Vly Mountain	4
27. Huntersfield Mountain	17
30. Lost Mountain	17
32. Ashland Pinnacle	17
41. Mount Richmond	19
45. Richtmyer Peak	20
50. Tower Mountain	11
50. Mount Pisgah	21
53. Mount Hayden	21
58. Ginseng Mountain	21
63. Mount Zoar	22
68. Windham High Peak	23
73. Acra Point	24
78. Thomas Cole	20
80. Black Dome	21
84. Black Head	23
87. Cairo Round Top	27
89. Parker Mountain	18

A R C 4th.

8. Slide Mountain	16
10. Panther Mountain	8
10. Mount Cornell	17
11. Wittenberg Mountain	16
15. High Point	24
26. Mount Pleasant	16
35. Mount Tremper	15
40. Mount Sheridan	10
41. Mount Sherril	5
57. Overlook Mountain	25
63. Indian Head	23

DEGREES.		MILES
65.	Twin Mountain	21
66.	Sugar Loaf	20
73.	Plateau Mountain	18
76.	High Peak	23
77.	Round Top	22
78.	Hunter Mountain	12
80.	South Mountain	24
88.	Colonel's Chair	11
88.	North Mountain	22

DISTANCE TABLE.

BLACK DOME MOUNTAIN

—TO ALL ITS CIRCUMAMBIENT—

CATSKILL PEAKS.

EXPLANATIONS.

Arc 1st, South to West. Arc 2d, North to West. Arc 3rd, North to East. Arc 4th, South to East.

ARC 1st.

Degrees.		Miles.
2.	Round Top	8
2.	Overlook Mountain	16
7.	Indian Head	14
12.	Twin Mountain	18
15.	Sugar Loaf	21
29.	Mt. Tobias	19

DEGREES.   **MILES**

ARC 2d.

DEGREES.		MILES
75.	Bloomberg Mountain	24
89.	Vly Mountain	20

ARC 3rd.

30.	Acra Point	3

ARC 4th.

2.	High Peak	9
25.	South Mountain	8
30.	North Mountain	6
60.	Black Head	2
74.	Cairo Round Top	7

CARRIAGE RATES.

The usual charge for one horse and carriage, to carry one or two persons a distance not to exceed three miles, and return, $1.00 For two horses and top wagon, suitable to carry from six to ten persons, with driver, $5.00 per day including board for horses and driver.

☞ CAUTION:— Beware of unprincipled persons who make it a business to meet all trains at the stations along the Ulster and Delaware Railroad and elsewhere, whose pretensions are to carry you to your destination and charge you exorbitantly for their services. It is often the case a traveler is "taken in" and duped by incredulous persons and made to pay $8.00 for riding a distance of seven or eight miles, when a first-class two or four horse coach will leave the station in five minutes, taking you over the same route for 50 cents. The traveler should remember that first-class covered stages, equipped with the best platform springs, and drawn by two to four horses, leave the station shortly after the arrival of all express trains, and run on nearly as fast time as private carriages, and for less than one-fourth the expense.

HEIGHTS OF THE PRINCIPAL MOUNTAINS OF THE CATSKILL RANGE.

	FEET.		FEET.
Balsam High Peak	4,000	Mt. Sheridan	2,490
Balsam Mountain	3,695	Mt. Utsyanthia	3,365
Big Indian Mountain	3,800	North Mountain	3,450
Black Dome	4,004	Overlook Mountain	3,300
Black Head	3,965	Pakataghkan Mountain	3,600
Colonel's Chair	3,200	Panther Mountain	3,800
Eagle Mountain	4,005	Parker Mountain	2,556
High Peak	3,809	Plateau Mountain	3,875
High Point	2,700	Richtmyer Peak	2,800
Hunter Mountain	4,052	Slide Mountain	4,220
Huntersfield Mountain	3,300	Summit Hill	2,485
Mt. Cornell	3,920	Vly Mountain	3,888
Mt. Hayden	2,775	Windham High Peak	3,500
Mt. Peakamoose	4,000	Wittenberg Mountain	3,824
Mt. Richmond	3,080		

EAGLE MOUNTAIN.

EAGLE MOUNTAIN was resently discovered to be the second highest mountain in Greene County. This mountain is easily reached from Shandaken and Pine Hill depots, on Ulster and Delaware Railroad. The distance from either depot to the top of the mountain is about five miles.

From Shandaken depot we pass Mr. F. B. Lament's Hotel at the right, and follow the left hand road up the Bushnellsville Clove a distance of 2¾ miles; turning again to the left, passing "Pleasant Home Boarding House," thence ascending a steep hill around a curve at the right, follow this road a distance of one mile, turn to the right and follow right hand road a short distance to Mr. John Rider's farm house; from here, Mr. Rider will furnish you a guide to the top of the mountain by way of a gradual ascending foot path on the western slope of the mountain.

Numerous fine and romantic views meet the eye on all sides while ascending the mountain.

Among many views, I shall mention a few of the romantic and picturesque: First, after having ascended a steep hill and near the forest, a fine and complete view of the Bushnellsville Clove, a portion of the central part of the Shandaken Valley, and an entire view of all the southern Catskill Peaks; also, a portion of the northern part of the Shawangunk Mountains are visible. Second, after having traveled a short distance up the mountain, to the right and but a short distance away is "Tin Ledge," the top of which is easily accessable on the western slope of the rocks.

From this ledge the views are so numerous and extensive as to be almost indescribable. The whole Summit Hill, including the "Horse Shoe" curve on the U. & D. R. R., and the "Summit House," lie in an unbroken vision as at our feet.

The scenery from the top of the mountain embraces the whole Cat-kill range and a large portion of the Shawangunk Mountains.

The route from Pine Hill depot is equally as interesting.

Taking the right hand road from the village and following it a distance of 3½ miles brings you to Mr Rider's residence, a farm house near the road at the left, thence proceed as heretofore described. This route passes along-side of the Birch Creek (an excellent trout stream) and the fine boarding houses of Mr. Hasbrouck's "Crystal Spring Cottage," and "Trout Brook House," C. C. Blodget, proprietor.

The "Piedfer Lead Mine," an excavation of 135 feet, is but a few rods from the road, and is found by following the first foot-path at the right, after having passed through two pieces of woods, the first a distance of one mile, and the second a distance of one-half mile; you will see several heaps of stones in the meadow at the right near the foot-path, following the foot-path by these stone heaps, and, up a steep hill in the woods a distance of thirty rods is the Lead Mine.

The views at the Led Mine are fine and well worth a visit.

The views as seen from Eagle Mountain are to numerous to be further described in this work.

Parties visiting the Catskills, and fail to ascend this "Towering King," miss the views when once seen will always be remembered as one of the great beauties of this "Switzerland of America."

1877.   ON THE CATSKILLS.   1881.

1,800 FEET ABOVE TIDE.

Shady Lawn House,

WESTKILL, GREENE COUNTY, NEW YORK.

A Shady, Cool, Home-like and Comfortable Retreat for the
SUMMER MONTHS.

SHADY LAWN is beautifully located, about fifteen minutes walk from the village of Westkill.

An unsurpassed view of Vly Mountain and other equally prominent Catskill Peaks.

Extensive, romantic and picturesque scenery.

Excursions to all principal points of interest can be made and return the same day. Daily Mail and Telegraph communications with all points. Connected with the house is a farm and dairy from which the table is supplied with an abundance of fresh vegetables, milk, cream and butter.

No Mutton served for Lamb, nor Old Hens for Chickens.
Accommodations for forty.   -   -   -   Terms reasonable.

Private carriage sent to depot if desired.

For circulars and terms address,

Chris. Riley,
Westkill, Greene Co., N. Y.

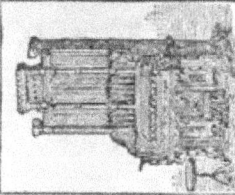